The Trials of Our Time

Md Rashid Alam

DISCLAIMER

This book is a work of fiction. The poet has tried best to edit and curate the content and made it plagiarism free.
All the poems in this book are unique.
In case of any plagiarism detected, the publisher will not be responsible. The poet will be solely responsible for his own content.

The opinions/ contents expressed in this book are solely of the poet and do not represent the opinions/ standings/ thoughts of the Publisher.

ACKNOWLEDGEMENT

I am extremely grateful to all the people who have been a part of my life even for the slightest. My family members, friends, teachers and the people who have played important role in the progress my life. Especially, my late father who had motivated me a lot learn more and experience new things which helped me to write my poems. Even the loss of my father gave tremendous courage and motivation write the poems.

I am thankful to my friends who have always been very critical to my work which helped me polish and improve my writing skill.

A special thanks to the publisher who believed in my work and helped me to publish this book.

Finally, to the readers who would embark on this adventure with me. Thank in advance.

Do reach out to me through social media. Your precious comments and constructive criticism would help me to improve my skill and motivate me to write more.

CONTENTS

In the Garden of the Creator

If you feel bad for what's happening around you,
Have patience no matter what extent things go.
Bow, kneel, prostrate and send your gratitude to the One
Who is the creator of both good and evil that you must know.
I believe this is a tumultuous time throwing us all into a great turmoil
But we should know that it is fostering a beautiful and peaceful future too
As we now know who is right and who is wrong; friends or foes.
There will be no back stabbing since the wrongdoers are coming out from their burrows.
Though, it may not be forgotten, how they squeezed the life out and left us in a miserable state.
Today is not different from that but tomorrow will be
When we shall all lie in the Garden which will bear witness to our deeds.

The Wanderer

I left behind the sun following the shadow,
There was so much in that illuminating light,
But I sought none sitting in a gloomy bungalow.
I've lost the endless bliss in momentarily delight.

I hear no birds chirping, no hearts beating,
And I could see the flowers wither away;
The trees have died of lamenting,
There's something coming on the way.

Far away in the fields, as I dream
With glittering eyes and exuberating fervour,
The aroma of his presence coming from the stream,
Carrying in his heart my cure.

Dilemma of Life

It has become a tedious journey without the
melodies;
Life is so surreal with infinite possibilities.
It might open a Pandora's Box of endless
bliss,
Or you might end up suffering vehemently in
the abyss.

I've been wandering in desolation
Looking for an oasis in the ocean.
Is it somewhere camouflaged;
Or is it nothing but a mirage?

Am I smitten by life's endless longing,
Or have I been dreaming?
The listlessness is stifling me
As if my other self is adamant to be free

Fallen Men

Their acts are not less than sorcery

Aren't they themselves responsible for their
species' mockery?

No wonder, among us they are residing,

In their tongue, what are they hiding?

Don't listen to them, they are not trustworthy

They are the suppliers of all the evil energy.

They are the profound city illusionists,

Nothing but fallacy they assist.

They are the Achilles without muscle,

But are capable of bringing the world into a
tussle.

But their purpose of origin was not so

Once they made the puissant to bow.

Why have they gone astray?

For their reformation, we can only pray.

Rotten Seeds

The loathsome seeds of hatred

That we're sowing in the garden,

No wonder would bring forth,

The fruits of intolerance;

Flower as dry as the sands in desert.

Bees whose hearts are sealed to produce honey.

There would not be any kind of productivity.

It would be a barren place

As if an apocalypse has just occurred.

The minds of people embedded with ideas

Of them being sage and us anarchists

Are the ignorant ones,

Because they've more follies

Than criminals of war.

Trial Of the Night

The odds of the night,
Creeping through the day.
Are we midst of a war?
Perpetual covetous hearts,
Broken and defeated souls;
Aren't clinging no words in their chests.
Deep concussions raise furors.
The delusion of the bogus
Well infected the gullible people
With their lurks and perks
Embedded with dogmas of faith.
Loving was easy back then,
There were no walls among us.
Broken walls have never been good to us,
But why do we yearn for a cleft now?
This is no more than a trial.
We would definitely pass through this mayhem;
There's no darkness without light.
This is the trial of the Night.

The Peacemakers

They will come, the peacemakers.

All well robed, smiling and amiable.

It's hard to recognize them.

When they find you all alone,

They ask you the most impertinent question;

'Who are you?'

And you would think it's just an identity quest.

But if you are not them,

They will torment you like hell;

You would beseech and scream for peace's sake,

But they won't listen to you.

And when they leave and if you survive,

You barely know who you are.

The Severed Kite

Flying up in the sky,
Have you ever seen a severed kite?
It looks arrogantly and laughs at the butterfly,
But unfortunately falls down after a short flight.

It will make no difference at all
Whether it flies or falls down.
Like a puppet or a doll
It was never on its own.

Rain is its enemy, wind's friend,
And the string is its soul.
But it will soon come to an end
Without fulfilling its goal.

Though it comes to a good hand
Who would mend, and it would fly again.
But fate takes it to the same end
As if its doom is certain.

The Wheel of Time

I've not lived through the ages,
Nor have I met the sages,
Though, I am a man of the Book,
But haven't turned its every pages.

Born with the aspirations,
To touch the sky and dive in the ocean;
Measure the Ganges, and the Nile
And to run a marathon.

I've not lived through the ages,
But seen people turning savages;
Crooked in their actions,
Neat and clean to us hiding their faces.

Gone are the days,
When honesty, justice, morality waged
Time's gone my friend,
The opposite nowadays better pays.

I've not lived through the ages.
'The worse is yet to come', they says.
The wheel of time has changed.
It's going through its different phases.

The Veils of Dignity

How could she have felt sitting

uncomfortably

In front of the men, old ones and elderly!

Isn't that the hypocrisy of the brutals,

Who decide what is right doing blind rituals.

She was questioned like a convict,

Not a word she creaked.

Her divine appearance made the people

believe,

She was perfect and naive.

Nobody cared what she wanted then,

Who knew what she strove within.

Once she dreamed to fly

But had to wear a veil of shy.

Aged sooner in servitude,

She always wanted a bit of solitude.

Nihilism

Dusk falls in the land
And we yearn for sunshine.
The hope is disappearing into the quicksand;
And life's become tedious as if we stuck in
the turbine.

There's no account of the tears,
As misfortune keeps lurking at the door,
All of us are in a dilemma
To whom we love, and to whom we adore.

Life has never been so nihilistic,
Left us wandering like an ascetic.

The Song of Prosperity

We need to sit and think right

What makes us unite.

Why is everything so fussed

When there's nothing to be rushed.

Though, the country's not absolutely fine

But why do we be the hurdle in hers shine.

There's only one life we have

Why don't we focus on things that make us

laugh.

There's already too much bitterness here

There's no more garbage to bear.

All the complexities that we have

It's high time to put them in rehab.

Time Machine

Sometimes I look back in time
In search of light and delight.
I've wandered places from hellish to divine
But found nothing chasing the infinite.

Trivial or terrible mistakes that I'd
committed
Good or jealous hearts that I'd broken
The cuss words that I said
To each and every beloved one.

I wish! I had a time machine
I could go back in time
Everything of others and mine
Set perfectly in no time.

An Ode to the Mother

So is she the precious One
The gift from the only One
For the intercession of everyone.
The flower of Eden
Came to adorn the desert.
Her presence brings prosperity in life
Her being spreads the aroma of paradise
Filled the world with her grace and beauty.
Her intercession shall make our ways easy.
Her prayer shall never be ignored
On the Day of Judgement.
Can such a person bring evil in society
Who was in the days of ignorance
Buried and burnt alive
For she was considered, Pandora
The cause of all evil.
Then came the most virtuous among us,
The most beloved of the Exalted One.
Restored the mother of the humanity
And taught the sapient,
The righteous way to treat her
For the endless bliss in the Worlds.

Gratitude

When I felt complacent,

You told me 'bout the unconquerable infinite.

I always thought 'bout the destination,

But you told me to live the way.

The way that is harsh and tough,

That I haven't seen you questioning about.

Your world is small,

 but it is beautiful and peopled.

You are the source of infinite

Love, compassion and friendship.

I owe you a great debt of gratitude

For holding my hand,

When I was feeling low and lost.

Dead Heart

It was like standing alone in the abyss of the
infinite space,
Not a single being seen all around, it hurts
There was utter silence, for a second
everything had stopped
Even my heart stopped palpitating,
I didn't understand a thing.
I never felt so helpless and restless.
Everything is gone, nothing left.
Ever since, I have been looking for that one
spark
That will bring back all the impulses to live
The life that people hope for its longevity.

Misfortune of the Good

So peculiar, the day it is!

It's neither a dilemma nor an enigma.

It is either frolic or tragic,

It's both honorary and a stigma.

It's the product of the society, so shall it bear.

The ignominy is at its peak.

They shout, 'carpe diem'

To the lifeless and the listless souls

The tumult of their trumpets has dried their

spirits.

There's no goodness in the good

Instead, there's much frenzy in our mood.

We're all indulged in frivolous acts of human

disgrace.

We've erased the line which distinguishes

good from evil with our stupefying acts of

valor.

Noor

I never talked to her
No one did so ever
She sat alone near the pool
That became her usual spot after school.

She read books under the leafy tree
Leaning against like a devotee
There came no one to bother her
Solitude cheered up her.

She's a ward of Mother Halima's
Told me one of the girls of her class.
And her name was Noor
That's what her friends called her at the
store.

The Lost Man

Where have we come

From the painless chorus of life

To this vehement and torturous cacophony?

I wish! I hadn't lost that serenity

And youthfulness of my innocence.

Have I lost everything?

And look, what remains is a vivid darkness.

Fumbling and stumbling, looking for something

That we have no idea, nada.

Once I was standing on the horizon

When everything was so pristine

But now it seems there's a screen in front of us;

Roaming around doing Sisyphean tasks.

Two Little Birds

Soaring through the bright sky

The two little birds perched on a wall

Flat on the top and built high.

It was a perfect stay to avoid the fall.

Picking and poking each other

With their bluntly sharp beaks.

And with restlessness, soon

They buried themselves with their usual plights.

Twittering and chirping, playing with utmost delight

Unaware of the impending misfortune

That they are going to face, as suddenly

A ferocious and evil vulture

Came flapping its wings

And caught the wing of one of the birds

with its beak and flew away.

The other could not do nothing

Because it happened in no time.

The Poor Dog

Have you not encountered such a dog

Free and aimless like a vagrant

Trying to cross the road

With its futile endeavour.

But much to its surprise

As never expected, the danger which lured it,

Got hit, crushed and killed by

A worthy driver who was in hurry

To reach somewhere earnestly

To do something efficacious

As if the fate of the world depended upon him.

Why should he have cared for the petty animal

Whose life was not worth the candle.

Graffiti on Wall

Gibberish, ticklish; Hindi and English

Deliberately painted nonsensical thoughts

Of naivety on classroom walls.

From 'God is great' to 'Sunny is an idiot'

Smeared and scribbled all over on the walls.

There's a rich profusion of words

Battling for syntactical and morphological

Coordination for connotative and denotative

Expression.

The thoughtless expression of thoughts

Painted, sketched and written at their leisure

Though, everything makes no sense to sensible

Person,

But to them, it's a fountain of pleasure.

Apocalypto

One day when everything will be gone;
On that dark and dismal day,
Unaware of dusk and dawn,
Being left over our fate to pray,
We all would be wandering around
Wondering over the hay.

When there's the end of the duality of our
thought,
Would begin an unwanted infirmity in our
esteemed liberal democracy.

When right and wrong wouldn't bother us.
Hope will fade away as the gust of wind and
Every living soul will dwell upon debris and
dungeons.

Shallow Strives

The story of their tantrum
Echoed in all direction with resonating drums
Filled the air with incongruous pride
With their discombobulated stride
And with their shallow minds
Embedded with facile strives.
What they achieved was nothing but zilch
And even if they wangled their way to
something,
they found nothing but a hindrance.

Tomorrow's India

From Kashmir to Kanyakumari
Each and every soul will merry.
They would look at each other with affection
And all would rise to perfection.
No one will remember the tyranny of our
enemy,
And we will forget our beliefs that once were
uncanny.
I wish my India to be like that
When we don't practice Tit for Tat.
Our hearts will be filled with the yearning
To love each other, not to despise.
I wish that all the darkness would go away,
When on every soul the sun rises.
That is the India, we all want to see,
An amalgamation of strength and tenderness,
Where promises are fulfilled, and dreams
come true.